The Eggs

by Mark Simons
illustrated by Janine Dawson

 **Harcourt**
SCHOOL PUBLISHERS

Printed in the United States of America

ISBN 10: 0-15-350348-3
ISBN 13: 978-0-15-350348-1

Ordering Options
ISBN 10: 0-15-350331-9 (Grade 1 Below-Level Collection)
ISBN 13: 978-0-15-350331-3 (Grade 1 Below-Level Collection)
ISBN 10: 0-15-357400-3 (package of 5)
ISBN 13: 978-0-15-357400-9 (package of 5)

2 3 4 5 6 7 8 9 10   179   15 14 13 12 11 10 09 08 07

Bess saw a hen. She went home with it.

The hen made a
nest. The hen could
make gold eggs!

"I'll sell the eggs,"
Bess said.

Bess made a shop.
Helen came to help.

They were good at selling.

Bess got the hen
food. There were
many eggs.

"I have many eggs!"
Bess was very happy
that night.